Spilling the Beans on...

FASHION

First published in 2001 by Miles Kelly Publishing,
Bardfield Centre, Great Bardfield, Essex CM7 4SL

Printed in Italy

ISBN 1-84236-012-4

24681097531

Cover design and illustration: Inc
Layout design: Mackerel

Spilling the Beans on...

FASHION

by Vicky Pepys

Illustrations   Martin Remphry

Miles Kelly
PUBLISHING

Contents

For my Mum, Joyce, and Dad, John Charles Geoffrey, who would have probably said how 'tickled' he was to see the Pepys name again in print.

About the Author

Vicky Pepys studied to be a fashion designer at St Martin's School of Art in London but always got told off for talking during class so got into PR where she was paid for doing just that! She worked for the designer Jasper Conran, fashion PR Lynne Franks and fashion show producer Mikel Rosen. She is now a freelance stylist involved in knitwear, shopping centres, photographic shoots, fashion shows and also copywriting.

Imagine

It's London Fashion Week, there's a huge marquee with over a thousand gold chairs with red velvet seats, a big white catwalk; photographers and TV cameras and crews are crammed in at each edge. The seats are full; on one side the crème de la crème of the British and International press, the fashion writers and stylists from the glossy magazines and all the big newspapers. On the other side the buyers from all the big stores in London, Paris and New York, boutique owners from all over Britain, and in the front row a smattering of pop stars and soap stars. They're all clutching the most sought after ticket for this season – a ticket for your first show.

The music starts, everyone's chatter is stilled to a hush and a single spotlight picks out a solitary supermodel figure just coming into view, gasps are heard – it is the most beautiful outfit anyone has ever seen!

Twenty minutes later, over 30 models have paraded your collection day and evening wear, sporty knitwear, cocktail dresses and coats with matching boots, handbags and hats. The final model appears dressed in a traditional bridal outfit to mark the end of the show and you are pulled onto the stage to be applauded and handed bouquets from all sides. You're surrounded by the press, you'll be in all the papers tomorrow and your appointment book is full with buyers wanting to stock your collection – you've made it!

Of course this doesn't happen to everyone who studies for a fashion career – but it happens to some. Look at Alexander McQueen, John Galliano or Stella McCartney; how did they get there? And what happens to those who don't get there? Where do they go and what do they do?

The first thing to ponder is, 'Am I sufficiently interested in fashion to make a career of it? I like clothes but do I live and breathe fashion like the top designers; do I have the dedication that they all have? Can I take the knocks?'

The best way to find out if you've got a chance is to answer the questions over the page:

1 Do you spend hours getting dressed, changing your mind four or five times, trying the same thing on this way and that to make it look different – only to be told when you get to the front door, 'You can't go out dressed like that'?

2 When you played with dolls (and that includes Action Man for the boys!), were you most particular about what they were dressed in, often altering their outfits or making up your own designs?

3 Do you often meet up with your mates, 'check out' what they're wearing

(thinking to yourself 'Those shoes would be better with red socks, or that cagoule would be funkier with a white T-shirt, half zipped and accessorized with a beanie hat'), and realize you haven't heard a single word they've said?

4 Do you spend hours poring over your mum's or big sister's fashion magazine, or window-shopping up and down the high street?

5 Have you ever tried to dress your pet?

If you've answered yes to all of these – you love fashion and this could be the career choice of a lifetime. But like everything, the business is a bit like a pyramid; not much space at the top and a long way to climb to get there. This book tells you how to get to the top and all about the other jobs that make up the world of fashion.

The next step

Well, you've got to start somewhere and that all depends what age you are. If you're reading this book, it's most likely you're at school and people are asking you what subjects you want to do and what you want to be when you 'grow up' (how irritating is that?!).

Bearing in mind you're interested in fashion, the likelihood is that you'll be doing art (essential for drawing and colour and form), probably IT (a lot of design is done with computers these days) and design and technology (learning how things go together). All subjects you do at school will have a use later on in your fashion career: maths is good for pattern cutting, English is good for impressing your bank manager, a foreign language is good for attending trade fairs and doing business abroad, even science has a use! Think of all the fabric technology that's used in sportswear!

The important thing is, don't think that fashion is all glamour and swanning around in chiffon calling everyone 'darling'. Successful designers are creative, have sound business sense, communication and people skills, and work very, very hard for most of the day and night.

So what do you want to do in fashion? It's good to recognize where your particular skills lie; and a starting point is deciding which part of it you'd like to work in.

A little quiz to help you with the decision:

You're at a family wedding. What's the first outfit you notice?

1 The Bride's

2 The Groom's

3 Everybody's shoes, handbags and hats

4 The ghastly one that your auntie is wearing for the fourth year running.

5 The page's and bridesmaid's

6 The groovy one, your elder cousin is wearing

7 You don't notice what people are wearing but you love talking, table decorations, the flowers and the food, the cars; in fact, the whole event.

8 The fact is you don't notice anybody's outfit except your own. You look fabulous and everyone keeps coming up to you to tell you how good you look

If you answered yes to 1, then you are veering towards ladies' fashion, which will give you the opportunity to design eveningwear and maybe a bit of bridal. This is all about designing to flatter and anything that's a bit fancy, using beautiful materials with lots of decoration.

If you answered yes to 2, then you might like to try formal menswear and tailoring. And that doesn't have to be boring – there's so many differences in suits: the collars, the buttons, the pockets, the linings, the weights and fabric compositions of the cloth.

If you answered yes to 3, then you might try being a shoe or accessory designer. You'll know yourself from your schoolmates how shoes change: how they can be out of date so quickly. And the shoes you're not allowed to wear for school – how outrageous are they? Even slippers are designed: think of all the new animal print mules – they're miles away from the old tartan ones with bobbles on!

If you answered yes to 4, and you've spent the entire wedding thinking how awful everyone looked and how much better they would have looked if you could have advised them, you might think of being a fashion editor or stylist. You'll then be able to write about what's in and what's out, predict the next big thing, and dress up models for photographic shoots so that they look exactly as you want them to look!

If you answered yes to 5, and you noticed what the children were wearing, then you have a fascination for tiny things, and would be ideally suited to working with childrenswear. Lots of things look cute when they are tiny: bright colours, appliqué, frills, patches and buttons, and the challenge is that they must be easy to get on and off, be comfortable and completely washable!

If you answered yes to 6, then you're interested in the latest fashions and would be good at designing for the younger market (up to age 25), as opposed to the older market, which is more classic, or even clubwear. You're probably up to date with all the latest looks, the bands, the magazines, the make-up and all things now. Designing is an ideal way to share your creative ideas.

If you answered yes to 7, then fashion isn't completely out, but you could be aiming for a career in fashion PR. That's where people organize fashion events and shows and campaigns for the designers for the world's press. They're the ones who spread the word about how fabulous a designer, or range of clothes, or a collection of shoes are, which is how we read about them in magazines and see them on television. The menu, the venue, the displays, the photography, the press packs and the goody bag to take away, that's all down to the PR.

If you answered yes to 8, then don't worry; you're not self-centred, you are just gorgeous and might like to think about modelling. Are you tall and graceful (guys as well!)? Do you look good in everything you wear? Have bundles of energy and manage to look cheerful even if you're miserable? Although becoming a model isn't really the route to designing, if you become one you'll get a tremendous insight into the business. You'll meet lots of the right people, learn about clothes, as well as travel the world and earn pots of money; and because it's a limited life (you may have to retire in your early twenties!), you can then study as a mature student (that means anyone over 21!).

So now you're thinking, 'Oh no, I never knew it was so complicated, there's too much to take in, there's too many choices'. It is hard, but it's such early days that there's plenty of time to think about it. You'll have noticed in department stores how the fashion sections are divided into types of fashion.

Broadly speaking:

Within Ladieswear there is:

✓ Casual, Formal, Clubwear, Eveningwear,

Sportswear, Swim/Resortwear, Bridal,
Uniform, Lingerie and Knitwear.

Within Menswear there is:

✓ Business/Formal, Casual/Weekend, Knitwear,
Clubwear, Sportswear, Uniform and Workwear.

Within Childrenswear there is:

✓ Party, Teen, Baby, Girls, Boys, Sportswear and
Schoolwear.

Look through your own wardrobe and see how
different types of outfits are easily
distinguishable into 'types' by their
fabric and their colour. Which
outfits do you prefer to wear
yourself? Which area do
you feel you know most
about or would like to
become an authority on?
Once you've sussed out
your own wardrobe, ask
permission to go through
someone else's and see if
you can do the same.

Do you feel you're a bit nearer to coming to a decision about your specialization? It's OK to have three or four areas of interest as well as just one or two. The top designers often have a couture line (the very beautiful garments costing thousands of pounds) as well as their main line. Some do a diffusion line (for younger cut and cheaper fabrics) and sometimes even just a T-shirt line to keep their name in the public eye. Just look on the perfume counters to see how many designers put their name and signature style to 'eau de toilette' and 'parfum'.

It's now time to think seriously about the educational route to fashion.

Starting out in style

The most obvious job in fashion, and the one you hear most about, is being a designer. This isn't to say it's the only job in fashion – we'll deal with others in a later chapter, but it's worth knowing what it involves so that you can begin to understand what the industry is all about.

This chapter is all about what a designer needs and how to become one.

To start with, you will know you are interested in fashion, but it may also be obvious to other people, particularly those at school. Your teachers may already know because of the way you try to customize your uniform.

For boys reading this, you probably have your shirt untucked, tie your tie very, very short with a big knot, and wear black jeans instead of regulation trousers – the key look is 'really don't care'.

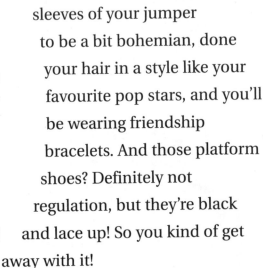

If you're a girl you've probably made your skirt much shorter than the regulation length, frayed the sleeves of your jumper to be a bit bohemian, done your hair in a style like your favourite pop stars, and you'll be wearing friendship bracelets. And those platform shoes? Definitely not regulation, but they're black and lace up! So you kind of get away with it!

(A bit of ancient history here: a friend of mine used to disguise his schoolcap by wearing it on

the back of his head and combing a
very large Elvis quiff with the help
of liquid soap (from the dispenser
in the loos, much cheaper than
wax or gel) to disguise it – it looked
good until it starting raining and foaming!)

So I'm interested in fashion. Does that mean I can
become a fashion designer? What do I need to be
able to do?

Your art teacher will probably be the one who's
noticed your fashion design potential most,
because you'll be a top art student – good at
drawing figures and textures with a good sense
of colour and pattern. And if you've ever done
sewing, you'll probably have amazed everyone
by whisking up an outfit in one lesson to wear at
the school dance that night.

Just because you're creative, doesn't mean you'll
make a good designer though.

You might have been asked by your best friend
to design and make a funky plastic party dress,
decorated with sequined mistletoe for a special

Christmas party. She's given you some money –
your first commission!

Somewhere along the way you decide that, as
the designer, you're allowed to make some
changes. You decide to ignore the mistletoe and
go for holly instead. Because the holly would
pierce the plastic, you make the frock from a
strong PVC tablecloth, so strong it stands up on
its own and is more expensive than the shower
curtain you'd originally discussed; and you
ignore your friend's phone calls because she's
disturbing your creative flow.

You arrive at her doorstep, the dress is prickly
and uncomfortable to wear, it's not what she

wanted and the party was last night – which was why she was trying to ring you!

A Giant Fashion Blunder! You were creative, yes! But you didn't give your friend, the Customer, what she wanted, at a price you agreed, and you were late – you missed the deadline!

And this is what the top designers have – Creativity and Imagination, Practical and Business Skills, and a great sense of Timing, which means that they always have the right stuff in the shops at the right time: early, and people are not ready for it, it's not the right season; late, and it's out of fashion!

Is that it then?

No, to pursue a career in fashion, you're going to need a degree or qualification of some kind from a college or university; this is the most recognized route and one that fashion houses require before they'll agree to see your amazing designs when you go for an interview.

A qualification like this proves to your future employers that not only do you have talent but you are able to follow instructions (known as a 'brief') and stick to those very important deadlines.

This 'talent' answering the 'brief' and 'being on time' formula is basically the gist of all the projects you'll be set through college, which is exactly the same, when you think about it, as homework – but homework that you'll probably like! What bliss!

Anyway back to the bit about after school. There are hundreds of sixth-form colleges/schools and universities all over the country that offer some sort of fashion qualification. To get onto one of these courses depends on your ability to 'win' a place (fashion is very popular and often oversubscribed), and which is your nearest college.

Most colleges and universities teach fashion in all its forms with a variety of 'projects' lasting approximately three weeks through your 2-, 3- or 4- year course; the higher the course the more complex the projects become. A basic design project could be just drawing and making the garment at a college, but would also involve market research, presentation, merchandizing and marketing on a university degree course. Remember, when you choose a college or university, you are also choosing a level of study.

Colleges and universities will only let you onto one of their courses if you've got an amazing portfolio (which is a folder crammed with all your best drawings and designs), have got the necessary qualifications and you do well in your interview.

So should I be starting to take subjects at school that are relevant?

Yes, you'll find out from your teachers all about which GCSEs or A levels and GNVQs to aim for to get onto an Arts Foundation Diploma, BTec or National Diploma course.

An Arts Foundation course is a year spent at a

college or university doing a variety of 'arty' subjects; you can have a go at a bit of everything – fine art, graphics, sculpture, photography and textile design are all covered. You 'specialize' in a subject in the final term and the tutors help you prepare your application and portfolio of work for the university course you want to apply for.

Just think, after this you'll be able to sculpt a shoe, wrap yourself in an exclusive bit of fabric, take a picture standing against a painting or piece of graphic work, develop it yourself and send it home to frighten your family!

When you're at the 'applying' stage, you get lots of help from your teachers or tutors in filling in all the forms. Teachers and tutors will also organize trips to different college and university campuses so that you can go along and see for yourself what it's like.

Where do I go to study for a fashion degree?

Fashion schools in colleges and universities are all over the country and sometimes specialize in different things.

There's lots of Knitting and Lingerie in the Midlands because of the local industry; Scotland is renowned for textile design, and you always hear about London courses, which get a lot of publicity, as some of their ex-students have become very famous designers.

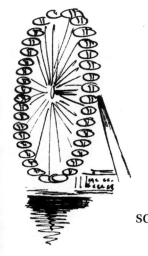

You apply to somewhere where, not only do you like the course, but you like the thought of living there as well; you will probably leave home to live in a flat, so this bit is very important.

When you go on a visit to a fashion department (they all have 'open days'), it's important to ask lots of questions like 'What kind of projects do you do?' Ask which projects involve people from the business, designers, manufacturers, fabric producers. Are there any famous ones from here? Ask about ex-students and what they are doing now. Talk to students who are there. Be very nosy! Ask if they do 'work experience' and what kinds of contacts they have in the industry.

You'll find a couple of places that you like and you'll apply to both and then you'll have to wait to see whether you've landed an interview, and you'll be getting your portfolio ready. This will have in it the best creative work you've ever done: drawing, painting, illustration, sketches, and even pictures of the woolly jumper you knitted for the family dog (with matching earmuffs)! Please don't attempt to take the dog with you to the interview! You've got enough problems carrying your portfolio!

Let's imagine that you've got an interview. You'll be ushered into the interview room and there'll be two or three tutors who will look through your work and ask you all sorts of questions about it and you. Some of the questions will seem relevant and some may not, but the tutors are trying to build up a picture of who you are and what you're about and what you would be like to teach.

What they are looking for is originality, creativity, positive attitude and enthusiasm. They will have seen probably 150 other potential students that week and, as there are only 40 places on the course, it's important that you stand out so they'll remember you later on. I still don't think it's a good idea to take the dog!

A period of time follows the interview that is nail bitingly, nerve wreckingly truly awful, as you wait to hear whether you're in (or out). This period of time is doubly awful if you are also waiting for exam results at the same time. With luck you get in and your results are amazing. Well done.

What's it like being a fashion student?

What stretches ahead of you now is 2, 3 or 4 years of intense study depending on which course you've decided to take; project after project after project, which are all so different, but you'll learn new skills all along the way. And it won't all be just designing: you've probably taken a course that combines a few other things as well, such as journalism, styling, fashion history, production, forecasting (also known as prediction of trends and nothing to do with horoscopes!), textile design or illustration.

One month you'll be doing projects about millinery, the next month tailoring, the next photography and packaging. You'll maybe have to design a range of winter coats using a rare form of wool woven in Tibet, research the history of the corset, or design fabrics using the influences of New York Graffiti. And you'll learn all about importing and exporting and how many

thousands of blouses a big factory can make in a week.

Your course might offer a trip to Paris to see the shows and fabric fairs, maybe well-known designers will visit to do a lecture and slide show or even set a project. They'll come along and mark your finished work, which is exciting and scary at the same time. It's very different talking to a real designer about your work rather than a teacher or tutor; they 'shoot from the hip' and tell you straight away if they think your designs will work or not.

But the most exciting thing is that, at the end of your time as a student, you might get to do your own student catwalk show. You'll probably have to design and make only about six outfits in total (as opposed to a designer with their own show, who has to make nearly a hundred!). But this is where you can get noticed as the next big thing, and not just for your designs. Your models might be all dressed in matching wigs, which shows your potential as a stylist; your music and choreography might show your talent as a show producer. You might have written a preview piece on the show for the local newspaper and offer potential as a fashion writer.

Fashion isn't just about designing, as you'll read in the following chapters; what's useful about all these courses is that you meet fashion people, learn about the industry all the way through and learn to live, breathe and talk fashion, even in your sleep! This will stand you in good stead, now that you're ready to be unleashed onto the fashion streets!

Route to the top

So when I've 'graduated', can I start designing then?

No, it isn't that easy. Even though you've got some skills, you haven't learned to use them professionally and there's still so much to learn from people in the business.

There are various routes designers can take, either working for themselves and designing under their own label, or as part of a team in a large clothing company, or being freelance, designing for many different labels.

For a designer to set up an own label, a lot of hard work is required plus a fair bit of money in the bank, to set up the premises and all the equipment necessary, not to mention employing all the people who are needed to help.

Designers spend ages thinking about a name for their company; some people use their own name or their name spelt in a fancy way, or choose something completely different.

Can you see your name being used as a design label?

Let's say, for example, that your name is Elizabeth Brown. You could play with your name to come up with something that sounds young and jolly, if you are doing daywear for instance, like 'Liz B' or 'Lizzy B' or, if you want to design classic or grand eveningwear, your company could be called 'Elizabeth' or 'The Brown Label'. You might even design a range of sunglasses with another name like 'Shades of Brown' or maybe 'Brown Eyes'.

Your stationery and swing tickets for the garments would reflect the character of the name.

A designer has to start by designing a first range of clothes called a 'collection'. Here in the UK designers begin by designing two collections a year: Spring/Summer and Autumn/Winter.

Spring/Summer collections have lots of dresses and T-shirts and shorts, maybe a raincoat, because it always rains in summer! And they are all in lightweight fabrics in nice bright colours and patterns. Sometimes designers do lots of swimwear and holiday clothes too.

Autumn/Winter clothes are made in heavy, warm fabrics; there are usually jumpers, and skirts and trousers, and coats with matching scarves and hats.

The designer has to come up with new designs six months before the shops will sell them, as they have to buy the fabric, get an order and get them made before delivering them to the shops so that we can buy them.

So who else does a designer need?

In their own design studio, designers will need:

A **pattern cutter** – who works on a big table next to the designer and is able to turn the designer's sketches into paper patterns and then cut them out in material.

A **sample machinist** – who sews and makes up the first 'sample' garments for a model to try on. Lots of alterations are done at this stage to get them absolutely perfect.

A **grader** – who works alongside the pattern cutter 'grading' the original pattern (making it in lots of different sizes), and making sure that all the patterns are ready for bulk production.

They also get ready the fabric and buttons and trims, e.g. feathers, ribbons and zips, before lots of the patterns are sent to a specialist factory.

A **production manager** – who will arrange and oversee the making of the garments in a factory with lots of machinists. These people will often visit the factory while everything is being made to check how things are going.

A **secretary** – who will do all the paperwork and letters, and deal with all the telephone calls and make appointments for the designer to meet fabric representatives, who bring round new colours and designs, and sales representatives from the big button and zip manufacturers.

A designer sometimes has to look through hundreds of different buttons, toggles, poppers and clips to find exactly the right thing – it can take hours!

An **accountant** – to make sure that the designer pays all the bills on time and that the designer is paid on time for any designs that are sold.

A **salesperson** – who will travel around with the designer's collection or make appointments in a showroom to show boutique and store owners, in the hope that they will buy something.

A **PR person** – who will make appointments to show the same collection to the fashion editors of the newspapers and magazines, in the hope that they will feature them. When a new designer comes on the scene, it is known as a 'launch' rather like the launch of a new perfume or car.

Who else will I need to know when I've designed my first collection and I'm ready to be 'launched' and have a fashion show?

A **Photographer** – who will photograph 10 or so best outfits from the designer's new collection, which will be used in preview articles by newspapers who are writing articles about the new season.

Designers work with photographers all the time – photographs can be sent to people to encourage them to come and see the collection. Sometimes the photographs are made into glossy brochures or used in advertising where they look even more impressive. Some photographers specialize in being catwalk photographers, who take pictures of the fashion shows around the world. These are sent to all the newspapers and magazines who are doing features on 'the newest looks'.

A **Fashion Editor** from a newspaper or magazine – who might want to interview designers to ask them what their influences are, where they find inspiration, and what kind of people they think will buy their clothes. To be featured in the papers prior to showing on the catwalk is very good publicity, and means that more people will be aware of a new designer and become interested in seeing their collection and eventually buying their clothes.

A **Fashion Show Producer** – who is a choreographer (shows models how to walk or dance on stage to music) and a good organizer. He/she organizes the whole event, helps choose the models, picks the music, lighting,

special effects and design of the catwalk to make the show an incredible spectacle, where the clothes look marvellous so that everyone will start talking about it!

A **Stylist** – who helps put the whole 'look' together and will organize shoes, tights, sunglasses and any other type of accessory, including ideas for props for on-stage. These can be anything from vases of flowers, astro-turf on the catwalk or even live poodles to accompany the models on stage!

A **Model Agency and Booker** – who 'books' models like booking an appointment, and through whom models are 'ordered'.

A 'casting' is arranged where all the models will visit the designer to try the clothes on and see if they fit and look OK. Designers always make clothes in what they call a sample size, which in this country is usually a size 10 for girls – that's why most models are that size. Some models are very tall and sometimes

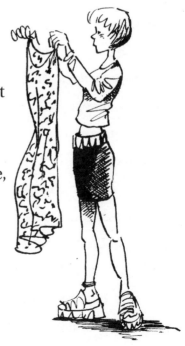

they just don't suit the designer's clothes, so it's important that they try things on.

A designer might also be looking for a particular 'look' of girl or boy as an overall theme, e.g. all brunettes, all long hair, or all shaved heads; 'fresh outdoors and healthy' or 'pale and interesting'. The model agency will listen to what the designer asks for and will send models along who answer to that description.

All the models chosen have to be able to walk in a special way, which involves stopping midway and at the end of the catwalk for people to see the clothes properly and to allow them to be photographed by all the photographers present. Catwalk walking isn't like real walking; it isn't

'hurrying to catch the bus walking', it's more like 'dream walking' – slowly swaying or dancing to the music and moving very elegantly. It's the kind of walking that can be done only in fashion shows – it looks very silly anywhere else but somehow looks really good in fashion circumstances!

Hairdressers and Make-up Artists – who are very talented people and who will make the clothes look even better by making the models very beautiful so that everything about the whole look is perfect.

These people will have talked to the designer about the type of look they want, e.g. Afro wigs, Geisha girl white face and red lips, hairbands with ringlets, fake-fur scrunchies, very glamorous, very space-age alien or very natural.

So many looks are possible with all the skills that these people possess. They spend a couple of hours before the show applying make-up and doing the hair of up to 30 models – and that's a lot of lipstick and hairdryers!

A **Buyer** – who represents a boutique or department store and who will make appointments with the designer or the sales person to buy some items from his or her collection. Buyers will look for designs that they know will sell in their shop or department; they spend all their time looking at clothes and will know all the latest trends. They are able to recognize which are the most important bits of each designer's collection and, most importantly, they have been observing the shopping habits of their customers for quite a few years and know what sells and what doesn't!

There must be lots of people you know who love certain things and hate others. Your Uncle Doug likes stripy jumpers. Auntie Anne might have a fondness for anything with feathers. You know

Mrs Henderson who lives opposite adores purple velvet. Your sister Diana likes funny patterned trousers. Your friend's mum Mrs Johnston likes very short skirts, and your cousin Dan likes anything as long as it's the latest designer label.

Well, they all go shopping somewhere and quite often they find a shop that seems to stock what they like. The kind of shop where you always know there'll be something that you want. That's because a buyer has noticed what you are looking for and keeps you in mind when they are placing new orders.

A typical order that a buyer might place would be 20 pairs of trousers (five pairs in size 10, five pairs in size 12, ten pairs in size 14 and five pairs in size 16), 20 tops (with that same breakdown), 30 dresses (ten in three of the most popular sizes) and ten coats (two small, four medium, four large). This is why they have to be good at maths, otherwise it gets very complicated!

They expect the clothes that they have ordered to be delivered to their shop at least a month before a season (Spring/Summer or Autumn/Winter) starts to be able to plan their in-store and window displays.

An **Agent** – who is like the sales person in the designer's studio. They usually work for themselves and sell clothes for lots of other designers too. They will take your collection and try to sell it to all the big shops and department stores abroad in cities like New York, Paris, Los Angeles and Tokyo. They have to be good at languages and dealing with different currencies, and not mind travelling all the time.

So now you've got this far in the book, you'll have realized that fashion isn't just about designers. There's a lot of people who make the fashion world go round – people with all sorts of skills and abilities with a fashion sense and a specialist knowledge of different areas within the industry. The next chapter is all about fashion without designing.

It's not all design

I want to be involved in fashion but I'm not interested in being a designer. What can I do?

Fashion affects a lot more things than you realize.

You can see fashion everywhere you look. And it doesn't just apply to clothes. Cars are fashionable – there are new cars appearing all the time with a new 'fashion colour' or interior. Certain toys are all the rage and sold out as soon as they hit the shelves. Small dogs that fit into your handbag are considered fashionable in Paris. Different pop groups are either very much 'in' or 'out'.

Fashion is a word we hear everyday, something is either 'old fashioned' or very 'now'. How many shops in the high street do you notice that have had a makeover with their interior, and possibly even their logo, redesigned to bring it more up to date – that's a kind of fashion too.

So there really are lots of things you can do that are related to fashion: there are different careers to give you skills that will enable you to work in the fashion world.

So, in alphabetical order, here are some examples of fashion careers you can have without ever even having to pick up a sketchpad!

Fabric Technologist

A Fabric Technologist doesn't sound very 'fashion-y'

or 'fashionable' at all does it? But it is one of the hottest jobs around. You won't be aware of them, but they are very important people in the fashion industry. They are the ones behind all the new developments in fabrics, all the weird and wonderful trendy material you see in the high street fashion and sports stores.

Look at any of your clothes and you'll see labels sewn in the back of the neck or down the side seam that tell you what it's made of and how to wash, iron or dry clean it. If you've not noticed those labels yet, then whoever does the washing in your house will be very aware of them. There are lots of fancy mixes and names like Polypropylene, Tencel, Lycra, Viscose, and ones that everyone, even your Gran, will be familiar with, like Nylon, Cotton and Wool.

All fabric is natural or man-made. You'll learn all about natural fabrics in geography. You'll know that cotton is grown in America, flax (linen) in India, silk from the silkworm from China, and wool from Australian or New Zealand sheep.

In chemistry or technology you'll learn about man-made fabrics. It's interesting to know things such as the fleece you wear on a weekend may well have started off as a plastic lemonade bottle – it's all made from the same stuff – oil!

Polypropylene, the trendy sports fabric of the moment, could well have been a carpet, but it is spun so fine that it almost resembles silk – the good thing about it is that it hates water but is breathable and it doesn't rot. Yuk!

Fabric technologists are finding out about things like this all the time and making sure that the fabrics will last when used in clothing. They are at the forefront of all fashion developments when you think about it – you can't make, design or sell the frock before you've got the fabric can you?

Budding fabric technologists will need to go to

college to get some qualifications – they either do courses that specialize in it or do a more general fashion course that includes some fabric technology.

You'll need to be good at the sciences for this one – particularly chemistry.

And at the end of all this you'll be ready to work with fabric manufacturers or be attached to a large clothing firm or a small team that works for lots of different companies. You'll sometimes work in laboratory conditions where fabrics are tested for moisture repellence, dye shedding and pilling (you know, when your jumper develops little bobbles all over it?) And you'll know all about the micro-organisms that can live in our clothes and make them rot and our shoes smell! Ugh!

Hair and Make–up Artist

There are lots of courses, some full time and some part time, to learn how to do hair and make-up. Most hairdressers start out as apprentices in a hair salon, and it takes quite a few years just to learn the basics of cutting and colouring hair.

To be a hair stylist or make-up artist associated with the world of fashion depends on the salon you work for. Many salons have 'session' stylists; This means that they are allowed time out of the salon to go to photographic shoots and fashion shows to do the hair of the models, style wigs or add extensions – whatever is required to create the look.

Lots of fashion hairdressers remain attached to a salon and represent them in national hair competitions where salons compete against each other for 'best hairdresser of the year' titles. These 'star' hairdressers do the hair of pop stars and film actresses, princesses and politicians, wives who don't have time to go to a salon themselves.

It's the same for make-up artists: often they start out working on a cosmetic counter doing a part time make-up course, until they become senior beauticians, and then they might decide to join an agency or they get a lucky break doing a fashion show and get noticed.

Some talented make-up artists can also do hair and *vice versa* – these are very important people to have around in the fashion business and quite often they set make-up trends themselves in the same way that designers set clothing trends.

There's always a bit of science involved and make-up artists and hairdressers have to learn all about the care and condition of hair and skin – if they don't know their stuff, then hair will fall out or spots will emerge!

Marketing

It's all very well designing fabulous clothes but, without marketing, a designer might remain only known by a handful of people.

Marketing people spend time and lots of money to give designers, make-up houses, perfume labels and lots of other things a much wider audience by advertising and promotion.

Marketing people come up with good ideas to 'sell' products with images – think of the billboard and magazine advertising you see and the glossy brochures in the best boutiques. Marketing people will have 'bought' the space, have come up with the 'concept' and the tag line (a unique phrase or description that you remember more than what the advert is trying to sell!) and put the whole package together.

Quite often they'll market the designer as well as the collection they've designed. They arrange 'deals' to make designer perfume or a range of tights, or publish a book – anything that gives the designer or fashion label a wider appeal and make them a household name.

Sometimes they arrange special promotions for fashion labels: 'Buy something from here and get a free entry into a lucky draw to win a pink sports car' or 'Buy three T shirts – get a fourth one free' and so on.

People in marketing usually come from a business school or college type of background or will have studied fashion marketing as an option on their fashion design course. They are usually one step ahead of others in ideas and are very aware of what the mood of the moment is.

Modelling

Models are everywhere we look – in magazines, on the telly, on billboards. They are the gorgeous people that advertise perfume, cars and even cold remedies. They appear in photographs in exotic locations and on the top designers' catwalks; they're at the best showbiz parties, they hang out with pop stars and some appear in films – what a life!

Of course that's the top models, the ones who are sometimes referred to as supermodels, and they earn pots of money. And they deserve every penny because they can't have a normal life! They have to be gorgeous all day and every day, and have to have so much energy it makes me feel tired just writing about it.

So what does a model actually do?

Models have to get up very early because they usually have to be somewhere that requires an early plane flight, train journey or car drive. They have to arrive on time, bright and breezy, for their modelling job and spend at least an hour being made up and having their hair done. They then spend at least eight hours in a studio or on location, having maybe 20 different outfits to change into, and they are expected to have lots of different expressions and poses so that the pictures don't all look the same. Why don't you try to do 27 different types of smiles in the mirror whilst looking gorgeous and see how hard it is?

On top of that they have to regularly check in with their 'booker', the person back at the model agency, to see what their next job is. They also have to attend lots of 'castings'. Imagine a building with queues of people down the entrance hall, coming out through the building, and down the street – that's what a casting can be like! A model is expected to attend castings to see potential clients, e.g. a clothing company, who are looking for four models for their Spring/Summer beachwear brochure. Location – Hawaii!

The model will queue with all the other models from all the different agencies to get a five-minute slot with the client who will look at them closely, talk to them about the job and look through their portfolio of pictures.

The clients are looking for models who will epitomize the image of their company or their advertising campaign, fit the size of their clothes, and hasn't just got one 'look'; in other words, someone who can show lots of facial expressions and poses. It's very important to have a sunny personality so that you will get on easily with the rest of the team on the photographic shoot. It can be very hard work and very tense, such as when the photographer's camera doesn't work for one reason or another, or it starts to pour with rain, or some of the clothes haven't turned up! And everybody has to remain cheerful!

Clients, whether they be designers, clothing companies, marketing or advertising agencies, all know what kind of model they are looking for and are quick to spot the face they want.

If you are picked for a job like this, it's the 'up-side' of the job; the chance to spend four/five days in Hawaii on the beach modelling sarongs and swimwear – hard work but fun at the same time.

And if you are not picked for this job, then this is the 'down-side' of modelling. You may go on 20 castings and not be picked for a single job, then

suddenly you are picked for three jobs on the go –
one in New York, one in Japan and one in Scotland
– you just never know what's going to happen
next!

So being a model is more about self-confidence
and the ability to 'sell yourself', not in pounds and
pence, but by putting yourself forward and not
being shy; that's how to get noticed.

Lots of successful models come from a drama or
dance background. They've probably been good at
sports and generally look fit. Not every model is
'pretty pretty' but most have what is described as
a striking look. It helps if you are tall; the reason
for this is that appearing on TV or in photographs
is always a bit of a shock, you always look bigger
width-ways than you actually are – so clothes look
better on models who are tall and slim (<u>not</u> thin).

So how do I become a model?

You might already be a child model and decide
that you enjoy it and might as well carry on. Your
child model agency may well have a 'grown-up
division' so you would in time progress that way.

For those just starting out there are lots of model competitions run through comics and magazines or fashion stores. Many of these are run in conjunction with the big London agencies who are constantly on the look out for new faces – this is called 'scouting'.

The best time to start enquiring directly to the agencies about modelling is when you're around the 14/15/16 age group. The big and reputable agencies have a 'new faces' section, who will be happy to make an appointment to see you once they've had a glimpse of a couple of snapshots of you. All the agencies advise against having expensive photographs taken because, if they accept you onto their books, they'll arrange to have special fashion pictures taken to put into your portfolio, known as 'tests'.

Many agencies have 'scouts' going around schools and colleges or fashion events – you often hear how models were 'discovered' and sometimes that's exactly what happens. A 'scout' will see a face and know immediately that he/she is the next best thing!

Of course, if you become a model at 15/16 years old, you'll only be able to work at first during the school holidays – there are laws to prevent you working more, for your own benefit, and you'll be accompanied by a chaperone. Good agencies look after young models and you'll be encouraged to take your parents/guardian along for your first interview.

If you're still a bit young to start thinking seriously about modelling, it's worth keeping an eye on the beauty pages in your magazines. You must learn to look after your skin and hair, take some regular exercise and eat healthily and sensibly, so that you are ready for the call when it comes.

Photography

You can study photography at school and college or university, and somewhere along the line you can get yourself a job as an assistant to an existing photographer. You will be loading film into cameras, carrying equipment, taking light readings etc. Working in a studio, you'll help set up lots of shots, putting up backdrops, holding lights and wind machines in place, and making the tea!

You may be lucky enough to get a job as a junior on a local newspaper picture desk or may even start as an assistant to a wedding photographer. You will then begin to learn about lighting, how to photograph people in studios and out on location, and you'll start to do fashion 'test' shots in your spare time.

As you learn to photograph clothes as well as people, you'll build up a portfolio to show editors, designers, and marketing and advertising people, and one day you'll have your first commission for a magazine, a brochure or an advertisement.

It'll take a few years to be commissioned by all the top magazines and designers but, if you have drive, ambition and extraordinary talent and technique, you'll get there!

Production Manager

If you become a Production Manager, you're organized, you're good with people, you're brilliant at doing eight things at once, and you've never been late for anything in your life.

It will be your job to make sure that the dresses, designed by the designer you work for, are manufactured and delivered into the stores and boutiques at the right time, and for the price that's been agreed with the buyer.

You will also need to understand all about the way the dress has been designed, what it is made of, and what buttons have been used, in case you find that the factory is putting red buttons on the blue dresses instead of on the green ones.

Typical problems you will deal with might include trousers being ready that are going to be sold as part of a suit, and the jackets haven't even been cut out yet! No boutique wants half a delivery! It's like having fish fingers and chips for tea, and then peas as a pudding!

Production managers learn their job by starting at the bottom, usually as a junior production assistant, so you'll have to apply directly to a fashion designer or manufacturer. There are, however, specialist courses at college and university for business studies and manufacturing processes that will give you a very good grounding.

PR (Public Relations)

PR people have been mentioned earlier on in the book, so you'll know that these are the people who help get designer's clothes and the designers themselves featured in newspapers, magazines, or on the telly and the radio.

PR people seem to spend all their time on the telephone talking to journalists, organizing the delivery of garments to photographic shoots, giving information on the garments, such as price, sizes, colourways, where is it sold, one London stockist, five provincial stockists, mail order, website address?

PR people get involved in lots of decision-making, working with the designers and the marketing people about advertising campaigns and brochures. They will use the photographs from a shoot for press packs (press releases and captioned photos) to send out to different fashion editors.

They need to be good at writing and coming up with innovative ways of how to present their 'story'.

PR people send out the invitations for fashion shows, arrange the seating plan, the goody bag (little presents and information packs on the seats), and they come up with ideas and arrange 'launches' and appearances throughout the rest of the year.

They often train like apprentices at an agency, where they are a junior account executive for a few years. They have a natural talent for being persuasive and friendly on the phone, are creative in their ideas and are efficient and organized. There are PR courses at business schools and colleges. On a general fashion design course you can learn about fashion PR itself. Like many of the jobs described here, you really begin to learn when you leave college. Colleges and universities give you an excellent grounding but it's at work that you really start to gain experience.

Purchaser

Like shopping big style?

Can you imagine spending thousands of pounds of someone else's money on fabric, buttons, sequins, ribbon, zips and other trims?

As a potential purchaser you will need to have a good head for figures.

Imagine – a gorgeous blouse has been designed that takes 1.27 metres of a kitten's paw print fabric. Seven buttons are needed for the front, and we'd better throw in a spare one in case one drops off. We need two small buttons for the cuffs, and then there are the 30 centimetres of ribbon to trim the collar; oh, and the embroidered kitten motif to sew onto the pocket.

Now the big question is, how much of everything do you need to make 2657 blouses? Have you got your calculator handy?

So now you've worked out all the raw materials you need, you'll have to order them from the suppliers. You have to make sure that they deliver the products you want, when you want them and, most importantly, at the best possible price. Don't forget you need everything in at the same time too – if you've forgotten the cuff buttons or the ribbon comes in late, no one will be able to make your blouses on time!

The subjects that will help you in your quest to become a purchaser are maths and English. Like most things described in this chapter, you will also learn a lot through experience, starting in a junior role and working your way up to becoming the head of purchasing in a large company.

Retail

How often do you envy someone who works in a shop surrounded by all the latest fashions?

To get to be a shop buyer or manager takes a lot of time and hard work and means starting at the bottom, maybe as a Saturday person or helping out in the school holidays. Some of the bigger chains do a lot of training in-store – that's when you see 'Opening 10.00am today – staff training in progress' signs on the door.

Working in a shop has an 'up' as well as a 'down' side. The 'up' side is that you get to see and understand all the latest trends straight from the designer; you get a chance to explain to, and influence, people who come in and need help choosing something to suit them. This is job satisfaction, when you've been able to help someone. And you'll probably get a chance to wear something trendy during the day as well!

The 'down' side is that you'll be on your feet all day, seem to be always unpacking boxes and putting things back on hangers which slip off as soon as someone walks past – and you have to smile all day!

As you progress and get more experience, you may fancy moving to a bigger and better boutique, or maybe to a department store that offers you more opportunity to become a manager of a particular department. You'll probably have the chance to suggest window displays or hold mini-fashion shows in the store and arrange designer visits.

You could train to become a buyer – lots of stores have courses in-store in order to train their own people or they may offer places to graduates who have been studying something related to retail.

And it usually all starts with a Saturday job. 'From small acorns mighty oaks do grow' is a well-known saying – you may well end up owning your own shop one day or even a chain of shops.

Shopping is such a personal thing and many boutiques reflect the tastes of the owners as well as the customers they expect through the door. Imagine if everything was the same – it would be a very boring world indeed!

Quality Controller

Imagine being in charge of making 2755 skirts – how do you make sure that each one is to the correct standard and that they don't vary from one to another? The answer is 'attention to detail' and a very good quality controller.

Quality controllers have to examine seams to make sure that the machinists have done a good job and that the garment is not going to fall apart. They spot every little mistake on a garment and make sure everything is perfect.

Quality controllers often work with or in, factories to keep 'standards of manufacture' high and consistent – you'll find them in lots of different industries.

They have very important jobs, as it is up to them to ensure that everything is produced exactly the same, all perfect, no buttons missing, no loose stitching and no trousers with one leg longer than the other!

To become someone as important as this means starting off at the bottom (like most jobs!) in a factory or warehouse, and being an apprentice and learning from others. There are college courses and night classes to help put you on the right track.

Textile Designer

In the fashion business you've got to have fabric in order to be able to design. Bearing in mind that clothes are designed six months ahead of being in the shops, textile designers have to work a whole year ahead so that they will have enough time to show their fabrics to the designers and then get them made up.

Even more complicated is the world of the yarn designers. They find it difficult to remember what year, season or day it is, as they have to design eighteen months ahead – they have to show their yarns to the textile designers who show to fashion designers who show to buyers who show to customers!

It's very complicated but, if you read it slowly, it all begins to make sense.

As an example let's look at wool.

Sheep are sheared, the wool is washed, dyed and spun, and then chosen by a textile designer to make an exclusive woven piece of cloth; the designer sells it to the fashion designer who makes a sample coat. That coat is shown at the fashion show and a buyer orders 20. More sheep have to be sheared, more fabric woven, more coats made and delivered to the shop for us to buy – phew! Does that make sense now?

Textile design is therefore very important when it comes to establishing new trends. There are four areas of specialism – weave, print, embellishment and knit. And below is the explanation of what all that means.

A typical woven type of fabric is cotton cloth. It is created by passing horizontal yarns under and over vertical yarns on a machine called a loom. If you've ever made a woven friendship bracelet or hairband on a kit that you got for Christmas – it's the same technique.

Weaving can be very colourful, textured and decorative, or it can be very plain, luxurious and sophisticated.

Another type of textile designer creates patterns and pictures to be printed onto hundreds of metres of cloth by screen-printing. If you go into the fabric and haberdashery shop or section of a department store, you'll see how many woven and printed fabrics there are.

If you look up the word *embellishment* in the dictionary, it says to beautify or to make more interesting, and that's another type of textile designer – someone who is good at very special sewing like embroidery. This kind of fabric is often used by the very top designers when they create dresses worth thousands of pounds. 'Haute couture' dresses are hand made to fit a particular person exactly, and are the kind of dresses you see film stars wearing to the Oscars! Luxurious threads or trimmings are applied or sewn onto the fabric to make it rich and special.

'Knit' textile design doesn't have to mean sitting in a chair for hours on end until your hands hurt! It can mean doing very complex, beautiful hand-knitted sweaters or it can mean machine knitting the finest cashmere. This type of textile design also applies to the creation of knitted fabrics.

Like weaving, this is the creation of lengths of fabric from yarns on a big industrial knitting machine but a different type of construction is used. Remember the labels in the back of the neck of your jumper or shirt? Creating fabrics is where all the mixing of the fibres and yarns happens.

Knitted fabrics usually have stretch, which makes them comfortable to wear; they are cut up and sewn into garments such as T-shirts and sportswear.

You will have to go to college or university to get a job as a textile designer, either on a specialist textile course or on a fashion course that offers textile design as a part of the timetable.

On a textile design course you will usually spend a period of time trying out all the different areas of textile design, and then you will specialize in one particular area. You'll have to learn about the 'science' and 'technical' bits: which types of yarns

are suited to which machines, which effects different techniques create, learning how to mix special dyes, and all the processes that are involved in creating a printed fabric length.

At the end of your training you may get a job working for a textile company, or you may become 'freelance' and produce lots of designs each season to sell directly to designers or fabric manufacturers.

Lots of fashion design companies now employ their own textile designers in order to produce exclusive fabric designs that none of their competitors will have.

Window Dressing

Window dressing is an art form with persuasive powers and one very much on 'public view'. Windows are the 'eyes' of the boutique or store and have to be interesting enough to make people want to go in and buy.

Many famous artists started doing window displays before they became famous – people like

Salvador Dali and David Hockney, so a high standard has already been set; but you don't have to be an artist to succeed.

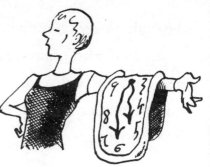

You'll need to be creative but also very practical at things like carpentry, or crafty with paper and fabrics. You'll always be on the look out for interesting and unusual props to display handbags or shoes, ties or tights; red lipsticks on red peppers, winter boots and shoes on piles of autumn leaves and so on.

You'll need to be very nimble as you'll be working in a very small space; you'll be a very careful person with a delicate touch so that you can re-connect a mannequin's legs without losing your grip and letting its face crash against the glass window pane!

Lots of colleges offer window display courses, or you could start off as an apprentice to an in-store team. Many sculpture or fine art students also like to try their hand at window displays, especially at the big London department stores.

So there are some of the jobs associated with fashion that you might be interested in looking into. There are many others that have been mentioned throughout the book so I hope it's given you an overall picture.

There's no harm in asking for more information about a specific job or qualification, whatever age you are. Apply directly to companies via the personnel manager, who'll probably send you a company brochure. Ask your teachers to arrange a visit to a nearby factory, or department store.

The 'ball is in your court' – or should that be 'the button is on your blouse' or ' the hem is in your hands'!

So what's the next step? Carry on reading and see...

On your way

If you're still reading this book, you are definitely and seriously interested in following fashion and choosing a career in something you've read about so far.

It's likely that you're still a bit young to be applying for college or university courses, and no one at school has mentioned much about fashion as an 'option' on your timetable, except for shouting *What do you think you look like? Pull those socks up! Tie your tie properly! Put your beret on the right way round! Roll back your sleeves! What's that sewn on the sleeve of your blazer?*

The thing is, you can start studying fashion now without it being on your timetable. You can start to do your own fashion education at home in your spare time, or with some like-minded friends – so you'll be well ahead of the game when the subject is offered as part of school or college study.

It's time to start right now!

Here's what you can do:

1 Experiment with your own clothes. Customize something old (get permission first). Jeans can be made into skirts. Trousers can become shorts. Long-sleeved shirts can become sleeveless and dyed pink in the washing machine (get help with this). Coats can become jackets by taking up the hem. Pictures can be painted on T-shirts with fabric paint, and Wellington boots can be sprayed. Just be very sure you definitely don't like, or won't ever wear again, the thing you are experimenting on. There's no

turning back on this one – there will be a lot of explaining to do if things go wrong! And there's no way you can replace something you 'borrow', and ruin, from someone else. This is also a good way of testing whether you're any good at sewing or drawing or following instructions! If it goes wrong, think to yourself 'It's not a problem – I would have chucked it out anyway'!

2 Start a scrapbook of the fashion pages in the newspapers and magazines you're allowed to cut up – you'll learn about which designers are 'in' and 'out' and what kinds of things they specialize in. Fashion editors often pick a theme for their pages like 'White Is The New Black'; in other words white clothes are going to be as popular as black clothes next winter. 'Get Ahead, Get A Hat', which will be all about how hats might be coming back into fashion. 'Make Your Wardrobe Work For You', might give tips about what to wear to look smart for work. You'll also notice hair and make-up trends from these pages as well, like 'Big Hair Is The Latest Big News' showing how using hair rollers, like they did in the seventies, is suddenly the new way to look! Or 'Luscious Lips For Christmas', about all the new red lipsticks on offer for the party season. You'll become much more aware of the different fashion seasons, and it might be an interesting idea to try to write a fashion piece for your school or club magazine, with some pictures of your friends all dressed up ready to go out.

This is a good way of seeing
if you can write
something interesting
about the fashion you
know about and have
noticed from your
friends and family.
You could also try
your interviewing skills
– have some questions
ready; a reporter must
never be tongue-tied!

3 Keep a little notebook about things you've
noticed people wearing that look good –
include people on the street. Notice what
pop stars wear on album covers and in
their videos, what actors and actresses in
films and presenters on the TV wear. This is
more about style than 'fashion' and how
people create their own looks. Sometimes
the look of an outfit can be changed

completely by adding a particular scarf or piece of jewellery, wearing different shoes or doing hair in a different way. You can experiment again with your own wardrobe by putting things together that have never been put together before, but just in a different way. See how many different looks you can get from a shirt – collar up, collar down, sleeves rolled up, sleeves unfastened and drooping, knotted at the waist, unbuttoned showing your vest, hung by the arms and worn round your neck, or what about as a turban?! It's all about not accepting anything on a hanger at face value – it's there to do whatever you want to do with it!

4 Look, really really look, at the way fashion shops display their clothes and group similar items together. Look at the window displays, the special offers that are available, the logos on the labels, the design of the carrier bags and the brochures they have near the till. Keep a memento box of all the examples of these things that you can collect and ask other people to save bits and pieces for you after they've been shopping. You'll begin to understand which shops appeal to which type of people. Look at how things are priced. Why is something priced at £9.99 more appealing than something at £10? Could it be something to do with the fact that it sounds like a bargain? You may know already which shops you prefer and now is the time to analyse why this is.

So you're on your way. There's lots of hard work ahead and the fashion world will be waiting for your unique originality and skills when you're ready. Whatever is 'in' now will be 'out' by then and your ideas could be the next big thing!

Good luck!